T0209222

A Call Girl with Her Clothes On

True Tales from a Night-Shift
Hospital Operator

COZETTE ZIMMERMAN

A CALL GIRL WITH HER CLOTHES ON
TRUE TALES FROM A NIGHT-SHIFT HOSPITAL OPERATOR

iUniverse books may be ordered through booksellers or by contacting:

iUniverse
1663 Liberty Drive
Bloomington, IN 47403
www.iuniverse.com
844-349-9409

Because of the dynamic nature of the internet, any web addresses or links contained in this book may have changed since publication and may no longer be valid. The views expressed in this work are solely those of the author and do not necessarily reflect the views of the publisher, and the publisher hereby disclaims any responsibility for them.

Any people depicted in stock imagery provided by Getty Images are models, and such images are being used for illustrative purposes only.
Certain stock imagery © Getty Images.

ISBN: 978-1-6632-2334-0 (sc)
ISBN: 978-1-6632-2333-3 (e)

Library of Congress Control Number: 2021910223

Print information available on the last page.

iUniverse rev. date: 07/12/2021

Dedicated to my parents, who always support me, even when my dreams and ambitions change, and to my patients, for without them, this book wouldn't have been possible

CONTENTS

INTRODUCTION

3:17 a.m. on a Saturday night

ME. [Hospital]. This is Roxy.

TWENTYISH-SOUNDING MALE. Yeah, I have a question. I need some advice.

ME. Sure, what's going on?

TWENTYISH-SOUNDING MALE. Yeah, so we've been drinking, and (*laughter in background*) my friend—we told him not to, but he did it anyway. He, uh (*more laughter*), broke a light bulb and ate it. We told him not to.

ME. Um …

TWENTYISH-SOUNDING MALE. So what do we do?

ME. Go to the emergency room. Now.

Starting in roughly the middle of 2019, I took a fairly generic job at a local (read: massive) hospital while working full-time on my college degree at the local (massive) state school. As far as I understand it, the job I applied for, interviewed for, and was hired for is a typical hospital job, albeit an underrecognized job. I became a call girl.

More specifically, I was a hospital phone operator working part-time on Friday and Saturday nights from 9:00 p.m. to 7:00 a.m. Every week, for nearly two years. But hey, someone's got to do it, and it paid benefits. Plus, I got to use the downtime between calls to do whatever I wanted to do, including study for exams, crochet massive blankets, and write this book. After about fifteen months in the night-shift-only part-time position, I transitioned to a partial-day-shift and partial-night-shift full-time position for three months and then a full-time day-shift position for about half a year.

The job was described as answering after-hours patients' phone calls, connecting the patients with doctors on call, answering guests (patients' friends') phone calls, and connecting guests with admitted patients. Furthermore, it included scheduling and rescheduling patients' appointments when patients called in and sorting and stuffing patient mail to be sent out later in the week. The job interview with my future boss and her counterparts implied that the job could get stressful and required occasional multitasking when multiple calls came in at once or when the doctors didn't answer immediately and there was a backlog of patients wanting to talk to doctors, but it usually was fairly laid-back and easy. During my training, my coworkers implied the same and weren't worried about my handling the job by myself, as I was flying through training. After roughly three weeks of training, I faced the weekend night shift alone.

In the first eight months, I experienced many calls but felt prepared enough to handle them with minimal panic. My motto was "Always keep your panic on the inside; cry later to your therapist." The calls were fairly regular and fairly routine—well, as routine as a medical emergency in the middle of the night can be. I handled the majority of my job easily and professionally, with many patients helped and no patient complaints. Then the coronavirus pandemic hit and changed everything. (Don't worry; there's an entire chapter devoted to those calls.) This book is dedicated to all the humorous, funny, and strange calls I received and the true way I handled the calls. I hope you enjoy these stories as much as I enjoy repeating them.

To clarify, I am not a licensed medical professional. Any life-saving advice I can offer or would suggest is from personal research

(Google) and random health facts I learned in different classes while studying for my degree. In this job, I was not allowed to give medical advice. Technically, I was not supposed to even tell people to go to the emergency room. But sometimes, at three o'clock in the morning, people really just needed a better adult to tell them what to do. It turned out I was that better adult. Unfortunately, people did not call back with updates on what happened, so I was often left confused and usually continued to make up an interesting backstory.

As I recalled, to the best of my abilities, these special, memorable phone calls, I did not edit them for sensitivity or for curse words, so they may contain adult language. User discretion is advised.

CHAPTER 1
Common Sense Ain't That Common

This chapter is for the people who called and made me question how some people survive in the wild. These questions and comments always made me stop and think, *What the actual fuck? How are you still breathing?* A small spoiler: my hospital is located in the southeastern part of the United States, a place not known for logical thinking or common sense, and oh man, did these patients prove that. I spent a lot of time wondering how the future of humanity is going to survive if many people don't understand what I consider to be medical common sense. These calls also gave me a reason to laugh on days when I felt down or overworked. After a shift during which I received these calls, I would immediately call my parents at seven o'clock in the morning (they love me) to share the stupidity of the medical world.

This chapter is also for some of the rudest people who ever felt the need to call me. I get it: patients have no patience. It's hard to wait your turn to talk, and you just want what you want when you want it, and that's right now. However, I am continually shocked at people who believe rudeness is the answer to everything and people who obviously didn't learn the Golden Rule in kindergarten. These people can make my blood boil with their audacity.

My most memorable call and the best call to start this book off with occurred at 3:17 a.m. on a Saturday night.

ME. [Hospital]. This is Roxy.

TWENTYISH-SOUNDING MALE. Yeah, I have a question. I need some advice.

ME. Sure, what's going on?

TWENTYISH-SOUNDING MALE. Yeah, so we've been drinking, and (*laughter in background*) my friend—we told him not to, but he did it anyway. He, uh (*more laughter*), broke a light bulb and ate it. We told him not to.

ME. Um ...

TWENTYISH-SOUNDING MALE. So what do we do?

ME. Go to the emergency room. Now.

TWENTYISH-SOUNDING MALE. Why? What's wrong? (*Laughter continues in the background.*)

ME. Light bulbs have chemicals in them and sharp glass; it could be cutting up his insides.

TWENTYISH-SOUNDING MALE. We told him not to. But then we turned around, and he ate it anyway.

ME. You still need to go to the emergency room. If not tonight, then at least go to an urgent care tomorrow.

TWENTYISH-SOUNDING MALE. OK, we'll do that. (*Speaking while hanging up the phone*) Dude, I fucking told you not to do that (*more laughter*).

I do not know the fate of this man or his friends. But if you are drunk, high, or having a moment of stupidity, do *not* eat a light bulb, especially if someone already told you it was a bad idea. Listen to him or her. You are no longer the captain of your own decisions.

11:53 p.m. on a Saturday night

ME. [Hospital]. This is Roxy.

ADULT MALE. Hey, I was wondering if you possibly knew what the cost of my [specific medication] is off the top of your head.

ME. Well, I'm not an insurance specialist, and the billing office won't be open until Monday.

ADULT MALE. Yeah, that's what my nurse on the floor just told me, but I'm doing my budgeting for the month, so I was trying to see if someone knew.

ME. Wait—you're in the hospital now?

ADULT MALE. Yeah, I've been here for a month now, and I'm going to be released on Monday. I was just doing my budgeting.

ME. Well, according to Google and GoodRX.com, it says the price can range from two dollars to two hundred dollars.

ADULT MALE. I didn't even think of Googling it. (*Gives ten-minute spiel about his hospital stay and medication and how his budget works with his family and his jobs.*) Well, thanks for listening. Sorry for talking your ear off. I'm just bored.

I hope the man got his medications covered, but unfortunately, he never called back with his insurance update. I still think about him whenever I go pick up my own medication.

Between 9:00 and 10:00 p.m. on a Friday night

ME. [Hospital]. This is Roxy.

YOUNG ADULT MALE. Yeah, I missed a phone call from this number.

ME. OK, did the caller leave a message?

YOUNG ADULT MALE. I don't think so.

ME. OK, about when did they call?

YOUNG ADULT MALE. I don't know.

ME. All righty, let's just look up your information and see if you have an upcoming appointment. What is your last name?

YOUNG ADULT MALE. (*Gives his name.*)

ME. Date of birth?

YOUNG ADULT MALE. (*Gives his date of birth.*)

ME. Great, and can you verify your address for me, please?

YOUNG ADULT MALE. Uhhh … (*Hesitates for at least twenty seconds.*) I don't know. Let me ask my mom, and I'll call y'all back. (*Hangs up.*)

It was an appointment reminder for neurosurgery!

The following call happened at least ten times per shift.

ME. [Hospital]. This is Roxy.

ADULT CALLER. I just received a phone call from there.

ME. Did they leave a message?

ADULT CALLER. I didn't check; I just called back.

ME. OK, do you see a doctor here?

ADULT CALLER. I'm not sure.

ME. OK, well, do you know of anyone who would be in the hospital?

ADULT CALLER. No, I have no friends.

ME. Let me look up your chart; maybe it was an appointment reminder.

ADULT CALLER. Well, I shouldn't have anything coming up. I'm feeling pretty OK.

Usually, these calls are about forgotten appointments the patients made six months ago.

The same call sometimes went as follows:

ME. [Hospital]. This is Roxy.

    ADULT CALLER. I just received a phone call from there.

ME. Did the caller leave a message?

ADULT CALLER. I don't know how to check.

ME. OK, do you see a doctor here?

ADULT CALLER. I'm not telling you.

ME. OK, well, do you know of anyone who would be in the hospital?

ADULT CALLER. Maybe this person, but I don't know how to spell their name.

ME. Well, unfortunately, we can't track outgoing calls, so hopefully they will call you back if they need to talk to you again.

The following was another scenario:

ME. [Hospital]. This is Roxy.

ADULT CALLER. I just received a phone call from there.

ME. Did the caller leave a message?

ADULT CALLER. It just said to call back.

ME. OK, do you see a doctor here?

ADULT CALLER. I see lots of doctors there.

ME. Is there a specific doctor you can think of?

ADULT CALLER. No, can't you just look me up and find a record of the message? [We can't do this, and usually the message isn't left in the chart, or the message was already sent electronically or left on the voice mail.]

ME. Let me look up your chart; maybe it was an appointment reminder.

ADULT CALLER. Oh, did I miss an appointment?

ME. [Hospital]. This is Roxy.

ADULT MALE OR FEMALE. I need to make an appointment or talk with my doctor, please.

ME. OK, what's your doctor's name?

ADULT MALE OR FEMALE. I don't remember.

ME. OK, what specialty are they with?

ADULT MALE OR FEMALE. Oh, I don't know what it's called.

ME. OK, what problem do you see them for?

ADULT MALE OR FEMALE, *with shock in his or her voice.* I'm not telling you.

ME. OK, well, unfortunately, I'm not able to redirect you to their office if you can't pinpoint their specialty or their name for me.

ADULT MALE OR FEMALE. Well, that's not helpful! You should know! (*Hangs up.*)

ME. [Hospital]. This is Roxy.

ADULT MALE OR FEMALE. I need to make an appointment or talk with my doctor, please.

ME. OK, what's your doctor's name?

ADULT MALE OR FEMALE. I don't remember.

ME. OK, what specialty are they with?

ADULT MALE OR FEMALE. Oh, I don't know what it's called.

ME. OK, what problem do you see them for?

ADULT MALE OR FEMALE. (*Gives incredibly detailed description that goes on for a few moments and is far more information than I need to know.*)

ME, *using all the skills and words I learned from my medical terminology class.* OK, hold on while I transfer you to that office.

COWORKER. [Hospital].

OLDER MALE. I need help finding the hospital.

COWORKER. (*Gives generic directions.*)

OLDER MALE. How about I tell you where I am, and you can direct me?

COWORKER. OK.

OLDER MALE. So I'm in a parking lot, and I see a sign that says [name of hospital]. How do I get to the [name of hospital] from here?

COWORKER. Sir, you are in our parking lot. You just need to enter the building.

I worry for this man's navigational skills. Sadly, he wasn't the only person to call with this particular problem.

ME. [Hospital]. This is Roxy.

ADULT FEMALE. I need to get to the office of Dr. (*garbled voice and lots of background static*).

ME. Could you please repeat that?

ADULT FEMALE. It's Dr. (*clearer but still lots of background noise*).

ME. Could you please spell the doctor's name for me?

ADULT FEMALE. I don't know. That's your job; you're supposed to know.

ME. (*Transfers her to psych so she can get some nice-people meds.*)

COWORKER. [Hospital]. How can I help you?

POTENTIAL PATIENT. Do you know if the school of dentistry or the dental school deals with teeth?

COWORKER. ...Yes, yes, they do.

CHAPTER 2
If You Have to Ask, You Need to Go to the ER

This chapter is all about the special people who don't know what an emergency is, need verification about what constitutes an emergency, or just need an adultier adult. If you have to ask what to do, the first step is to always panic, and the second step is to get your butt straight to the ER. If you think it is an emergency, it most likely is, unless you're a hypochondriac, in which case it can probably wait until daylight hours.

Word of warning: many of my fellow weekend and overnight call center employees were in college. In my midtwenties, I was one of the oldest people answering the phones. So if you need to call to verify if something is an emergency, you are depending on a bunch of teenagers giving advice. Best of luck.

6:34 a.m.
ME. [Hospital]. This is Roxy.
YOUNG-ADULT-SOUNDING FEMALE. Yeah, so I'm bleeding.
ME. OK, where are you bleeding?

YOUNG-ADULT-SOUNDING FEMALE. So I had some bleeding in (*unintelligible*) but not a lot.

ME. Do you see a doctor here?

YOUNG-ADULT-SOUNDING FEMALE. Yeah.

ME. OK, can I get your name and birth date?

YOUNG-ADULT-SOUNDING FEMALE. (*Provides information.*)

Two minutes later

ME. So where did you say you were bleeding from?

YOUNG-ADULT-SOUNDING FEMALE. My vagina. I woke up, and there's blood. I'm pregnant.

ME. Let me page the ob-gyn on call.

Approximately two o'clock in the morning

ME. [Hospital]. This is Roxy.

ADULT FEMALE. Yeah, I'm in the middle of a miscarriage, and I don't know what to do.

ME. Let me page the ob-gyn on call.

Some unsolicited common medical advice: if you are having any kind of miscarriage or pregnancy-related bleeding, please go to the ER. The staff will help you.

Approximately three o'clock in the morning

ME. [Hospital]. This is Roxy.

ADULT MOTHER. My son is less than a month old and had open-heart surgery last week because he has tetralogy of Fallot, and he just turned blue in his sleep. What do I do?

ME, *to myself. Panic.*

ME, *out loud.* Let me page the doctor on call for you.

11:26 p.m. on a Saturday night

ME. [Hospital]. This is Roxy.

MAN. My girlfriend's been shot!

ME, *internally screaming.* Have you called an ambulance?

MAN. No, my wife shot my girlfriend.

ME. Have you called an ambulance?

MAN. No, I need the police!

ME. Sir, I'm going to place you on a brief hold while I call 911 for you and connect you. (*Places the man on hold and calls 911 from the second line.*)

911. 911. Is this an emergency?

ME. Hi. This is Roxy from [hospital] health line, and, Operator, we just received a strange phone call. (*Explains the details of the call.*) We didn't know what to do, so we called you. And, well, it looks like the man hung up on the other line.

911. OK, did you get a phone number or name or address?

ME. No, unfortunately, this is the first time we've received a call like this, but I want to inform you so you guys can be aware and ready if he calls you.

911. OK, I'll write down an information report and pass it along to the officers so they are aware. (*Hangs up.*)

One minute later

HOSPITAL SECURITY. Did you just call 911 from this number?

ME. Yes. (*Explains situation.*)

HOSPITAL SECURITY. That's very weird. We just wanted to check to make sure the person placing the call is OK. We get automated notices when 911 is called from hospital property.

This man never called back, but my boss managed to trace the phone call and provide the information to the police. Lesson from that day: always keep your affairs secret and your guns hidden. Or maybe just don't have an affair.

4:00 a.m. on a Sunday morning
ME. [Hospital]. This is Roxy.
YOUNG ADULT FEMALE. So we've been drinking, and my friend just started throwing up blood.
ME. You need to take her to the emergency room now.
YOUNG ADULT FEMALE. Well, she says this has happened to her a couple of times before, and it's fine.
ME. I'm not a licensed medical professional, but in my experience, this is not fine.

Between 3:00 and 4:00 a.m. on a Sunday morning
ME. [Hospital]. This is Roxy.
YOUNG WOMAN IN HER TWENTIES. Are these calls monitored?
ME. We do record all of our phone calls in case something were to happen or we need to follow up with a patient.
YOUNG WOMAN. No, is someone listening to these, and will they come arrest me?
ME. Not that I am aware of. Our first priority is to help people with medical emergencies. We aren't monitoring calls to actively get people into trouble.

YOUNG WOMAN. OK, so I have a question. I am currently on [antidepressant], and I was drinking at a party, and I decided to do just a little bit of coke. But then I was concerned, and I googled it, and it said mixing cocaine with [antidepressant] could make my brain swell and cause intense damage. It was just a little bit of coke though.

ME. Well, I'm not a licensed medical professional, but I can't recommend doing illegal drugs while on prescription medication; however, I don't believe you are in immediate harm.

YOUNG WOMAN. I'm starting to panic, and I'm concerned I'm going to die in my sleep, but I don't want the police to arrest me in the emergency room.

ME. The police are not here to immediately arrest you. They would arrest you if you started dealing drugs in the ER in front of them or started doing drugs in front of them, but they aren't going to come after you for being concerned about a potential reaction.

YOUNG WOMAN. I don't feel anything weird now, but I'm scared. I shouldn't have googled it.

ME. Instead of potentially getting a large ER bill, how about if you drink a ton of water and take some Tylenol? Then, in the morning, if you feel like you are having a reaction to the drugs mixing, you could go to the urgent care.

YOUNG WOMAN. OK, that sounds great! I've drunk tons of water already, but Google said this was the first reaction, so now I'm really scared.

ME. Again, I can't recommend that you mix illegal drugs with alcohol and prescription medication, but I don't think that doing cocaine once will immediately make your brain explode. However, again, I am not a licensed medical professional.

YOUNG WOMAN. OK, I understand. I'm so anxious now, but I do feel a little better.

ME. Fantastic. We are always here to help if you need anything, but just self-monitor, and try not to do any more illegal drugs.

YOUNG WOMAN. I won't! I didn't even feel high or anything good, so I won't be doing this again. Thank you. Good night!

Folks, please do not do illegal drugs, even if it is just a little bit of coke. There is a reason these drugs are illegal!

CHAPTER 3
If I Answer One More Call like This, I Will Scream

People can be repetitive, thoughtless, and sometimes downright rude. Unfortunately, there seems to be a curfew on manners, and people also like to take their stress out on the unknown voice on the other end of the line. I understand this frustration, and I once yelled at a phone operator because I didn't feel heard. I get it: medical emergencies are scary, tensions are high, and all the bad stuff happens at night. But darn it, I am a human being too, and some of these calls hurt my feelings or frustrated me to no end, because I usually received these calls immediately after a stressful call or one that required more energy and effort on my part. My dad told me not to take it personally, but everything is personal at three o'clock in the morning.

ME. [Hospital]. This is Roxy.
MIDDLE-AGED-SOUNDING FEMALE. Yeah, I don't care what your name is. Just transfer me to [patient].

The following phone call was a weekly, if not daily, occurrence:

ME. [Hospital]. This is Roxy.

ADULT, *speaking with a ridiculously loud TV on in the background.* I can't hear you.

ME, *louder.* [Hospital]. This is Roxy.

ADULT, *speaking with the TV still so loud that I can understand the dialogue.* What?

ME, *yelling.* [Hospital]! This is Roxy!

ADULT. (*TV volume has not gone down.*) I'll call back when I can hear you.

Only one of us has the ability to change the caller's TV volume and phone volume, and it sure as heck isn't me.

ME. [Hospital]. This is Roxy.

ADULT. Yeah, do you have a patient named John there?

ME. What's his last name?

ADULT. Well, I don't know. We just call him John. That might not be his real name. (*Speaks to someone in the background.*) Honey, what's John's real name? (*Refers back to me.*) I'll just text him. (*Hangs up.*)

ME. [Hospital]. This is Roxy.

ADULT MOTHER, *with a baby screaming into the phone.* My child is having some medical issues and—

ME. I'm sorry, but I can't hear you.

ADULT MOTHER, *with baby still screaming and now screaming herself.* I said my child is having a medical emergency!

Between 4:00 and 5:00 a.m. on a Saturday morning

ME. [Hospital]. This is Roxy.

ADULT CALLER. I just saw that Jane posted on Facebook that she is in the emergency room now. Can I talk to her to see what's going on?

ME. I'm not seeing any patient by that name in our system. When did she inform you of this?

ADULT CALLER. She just posted about ten to fifteen minutes ago.

ME. Well, unfortunately, because she is not showing up in my system, I don't have the ability to transfer this phone call.

ADULT CALLER, *beginning to sound frustrated.* I *know* she's in there, so you have to let me talk to her!

ME. At this point in time, we don't have a registered patient by that name. It will take some time to get her registered. You could always talk to her on Facebook to see if she knows what's going on and if she can update you until she is registered.

ADULT CALLER. No, it's early; I don't want to bother her if she is unwell.

ME, *internally. I am very confused about this person's complete turnaround in attitude.*

Sometime after business hours, usually around midnight or so

ME. [Hospital]. This is Roxy.

CALLER. I was wondering what hotels are close to that hospital.

ME, *thoroughly surprised by the question.* I don't know off the top of my head, but I can google it for you. Google shows that there are three hotels near our location.

CALLER. And what are those hotels? Can I walk to the hospital from any of them?

ME. I'm not sure. I'm at an off-site location and don't usually stay at the hotels around here.

CALLER. All right, well, I will just google it myself and call them to see what they say.

ME, *to myself. Why did you call me if you're just going to do the same thing I did?*

Between 11:00 p.m. and 2:00 a.m. on a Friday night

ME. [Hospital]. This is Roxy.

CALLER. I'm coming from [name of city three hours away by car], and I was wondering what the closest airport is.

ME. If I were you, I would drive my own car or take a charter bus; it's cheaper and easier.

CALLER. I want to fly. I see there are two airports close to you, according to Google.

ME. [Airport 1] is very small and does not have many flights, and [Airport 2] is about a forty-five-minute drive away.

CALLER. Isn't there anything closer? (*Continues this conversation in circles for five to ten more minutes.*) Well, if you were in my position, what is the most direct route you would take to get to the hospital?

ME, *fed up.* Sir, I would drive because I live five minutes away from the hospital and wouldn't want to waste money on flying. If there isn't anything else I can help you with, I will have to end this call.

Approximately ten thirty on a Saturday night

ME. [Hospital]. This is Roxy.

OLDER WOMAN. I have an appointment next Thursday, and I was calling to get driving directions to the hospital from [a city two hours away].

ME. I'm sorry, ma'am, but you will have to call back during the week or on the morning of your appointment when you are close to the facility to get more accurate directions.

OLDER WOMAN. Oh, OK. I was just trying to be prepared. Thank you.

In this case, I thought, *Why did you feel the need to call five days in advance for driving directions that are mailed to you and are available on Google?*

The following happened frequently in the middle of the night:

ME. [Hospital]. This is Roxy.

PATIENT'S VISITOR. Yes, I am lost, and I need help in getting to the hospital.

ME. Do you see any specific signs telling you where you are?

PATIENT'S VISITOR, *annoyed and short-tempered.* No! I'm from out of town, and I've never been here! I don't know what I'm looking for!

ME. How did you get this number then?

PATIENT'S VISITOR. I googled it, of course!

Folks, if you can google a phone number, just use your GPS. It's much harder for an operator to try to guess where you are based on vague descriptions as he or she looks at Google Maps. Also, most hospitals have signs from main highways directing you to the hospital. Emergency services are pretty good at letting people know where to find them!

The following call happened at least five times, as I documented in our online notes system. It most likely happened closer to ten times. All of these calls happened between midnight and four o'clock in the morning on a weekend night.

ME. [Hospital]. This is Roxy.

FREQUENT CALLER. This is [patient], and I need y'all to send an ambulance to come get me. I am severely constipated, and I need to be seen.

ME. Is there a relative who could drive you up here?

FREQUENT CALLER, *angry and loud.* No! I can't drive, and no one else is available to drive, and the transfer bus won't take me that far. They only take me to [affiliated hospital that is thirty minutes away], but I don't like going there, because they won't help me, and they call me a faker and think I'm making this up.

ME. According to the notes left by the doctors, they do not have the ability to transport you here by ambulance for this problem, and you will have to call during clinic daytime hours for medical treatment for this issue.

FREQUENT CALLER. Well, aren't you useless? (*Hangs up.*)

I couldn't help but think, *I'm sorry that I won't page a doctor for an issue that you can get over-the-counter medication for. Drink some prune juice, and eat more fiber if this is such an extreme issue that you feel the need to call us in the middle of the night.*

The lady below didn't call on the weekends as much as she did during weekdays, but she was memorable the two times I spoke with her. My coworker said the lady called roughly two to four times a week during her shifts, and this conversation was repeated.

Approximately two o'clock in the morning
ME. [Hospital]. This is Roxy.
FREQUENT CALLER. Is this [my real name]?
ME. Yes, how can I help you?
FREQUENT CALLER. I remember you. You're always so nice and so kind to me, even if you can't help me with what I need.
ME, *concerned*. Are you having a medical emergency? Is there a doctor I can connect you with?
FREQUENT CALLER. Oh no. I don't want to bother him; he's on vacation, and this isn't serious enough to wake someone else up for.
ME, *confused*. OK, how can I help you?
FREQUENT CALLER. (*Launches into a fifteen- to thirty-minute-long monologue, talking about her favorite movie, her cats, and dreams of me standing in a sunflower field and holding a pink parasol to shade my white skin; asking questions about my dating life; and giving explanations for why she isn't dating and some personal details about her medical problems.*)

ME, *ready for a small break from her rambling.* Ma'am, is there something I can help you with this evening? Unfortunately, I'm the only one on the phone, and there are other people I need to help.

FREQUENT CALLER. No, I just was feeling lonely and needed to talk. You're always so nice and helpful toward me.

ME. All right then, I'm going to have to end this call if there isn't a medical emergency I can help you with.

I should feel lucky that she kept it brief with me. She has spent about forty-five minutes to more than an hour just talking at my coworker and tying up the phone lines.

CHAPTER 4
Why Did You Wait until the Weekend to Call?

Sometimes I think there's a whole group of people who don't know how to read a calendar or tell time. Many people seem to like to wait until the weekend to schedule all their important doctor visits, do the things on their to-do lists that they have been putting off all week, or even just mindlessly research medical procedures and ask questions about upcoming procedures. I'm sure this is an American sentiment of expecting everything to be open and available twenty-four hours a day, seven days a week, thanks to the store models of Walmart and online shopping. But many doctors' offices and clinics stick with working hours of Monday through Friday, 8:00 a.m. to 5:00 p.m., which means the appointment schedulers, main doctors, nurses, and people with prescription licenses go home and get to enjoy their time away from patients on the weekend.

Unfortunately, there are many people who wait until the weekend or just plain forget about their medical issues until it is either too late to give effective immediate help or until the operator has to page a doctor. This chapter is devoted to all the people who need to learn to read a clock and a calendar and to understand that their doctors do not just wait around for them to call.

Between 2:00 and 4:00 a.m. on a Sunday morning

ME. [Hospital]. This is Roxy.

FEMALE NURSE. Good morning. Yes, we have a patient in our nursing home facility who died, and the family wants to donate the body, and we were wondering how to do that.

ME, *befuddled*. Um, I've never dealt with one of these calls, so let me do some digging.

FEMALE NURSE. That's OK. Take your time. We didn't know what to do either.

ME. (*Calls house supervisor.*) Hey, so I have a weird question. How does someone donate a family member's body to our hospital?

HOUSE SUPERVISOR, *also befuddled*. They call the human gift registry number during weekday business hours.

ME. OK, is there any way they can donate or transport the body to our hospital tonight?

HOUSE SUPERVISOR. Um, no, it's not immediate or an emergency at this point. They can wait till Monday.

ME. OK, great. I will tell them. (*Connects back to original caller.*) Yes, hi. So to donate a body to our facility, you need to call the human gift registry during weekday business hours, and they will give you the protocol.

FEMALE NURSE. That sounds logical. We just had the son telling us to immediately donate the body, and they didn't want to deal with it.

I personally would have waited a day to mourn or called during the week, when most of the business world is awake, but OK, sir.

The following call happened multiple times over the weekends, at any point during the day. I understand addiction is a difficult battle to fight, and if you need medical intervention to help fight it, then I support you. But hospitals legally cannot prescribe any controlled substances during off-hours or overnight hours to patients over the phone. If you are in that much pain or dying, seek emergency medical treatment at the closest facility, and they will help you.

ME. [Hospital]. This is Roxy.

PATIENT. Yes, I was supposed to have a [Suboxone, oxycodone, Valium, Vicodin, morphine, or other addictive controlled substance] script called in, but the pharmacy says they never received it. Can I talk to my doctor?

ME. Sure, hold on while I page the psychiatric doctor on call.

There were typically a few medical professional responses, including the following:

PROVIDER RESPONSE 1. I don't have a DEA number or prescription license to give this person the medication, so they will have to wait until Monday before that provider comes into the clinic.

ME. OK, I need you to tell them that, because I legally cannot.

PROVIDER RESPONSE 2. They missed their mandated drug therapy session, and we cannot give them anything until they present to us in person.

ME. All right, I need you to tell them that, because I legally cannot.

PROVIDER RESPONSE 2. Sure, go ahead and connect me.

PATIENT, *unsettled*. But I can't go this long without my medications! I will go into withdrawal!

PROVIDER RESPONSE 2. You are always more than welcome to come to the emergency room if you are having that many issues, and we can evaluate you and admit you to the hospital if necessary.

PATIENT. I can't do that tonight! I don't have time!

PROVIDER RESPONSE 3. We are no longer providing this patient with these substances, because they have abused them in the past.

ME. All right, I need you to tell them that, because I legally cannot.

PROVIDER RESPONSE 3. Sure, go ahead and connect me.

PATIENT. But I'm in pain, and I'm suffering. Do you not understand? I might die if I have to be in this kind of pain for long! I need my meds!

PROVIDER RESPONSE 3. You are always more than welcome to come to the emergency room if you are having that many issues, and we can evaluate you and admit you to the hospital if necessary.

PATIENT. I can't do that. I don't have a car, and no one will drive me to the hospital, and the ambulances say I'm fine enough and won't transport me.

PROVIDER RESPONSE 3. I'm sorry to hear that, but at this point, it will be up to you to seek face-to-face medical attention if you need help.

PATIENT. (*Usually angry and screaming, hangs up.*)

PROVIDER RESPONSE 4, *overwhelmed and annoyed*. We already told them no, we won't be giving them any more of this medication.

ME. All right, I need you to tell them that, because I legally cannot.

PROVIDER RESPONSE 4. Sure, go ahead and connect me.

PATIENT. Hi. I—

PROVIDER RESPONSE 4. No. (*Hangs up.*)

I'm not personally a parent, so I don't quite understand all the fears that go along with newborns, but I hope I will not be like the parents in these next few stories.

Sometime between midnight and 3:00 a.m. on a Sunday morning
ME. [Hospital]. This is Roxy.

PARENT OF PATIENT. Yes, my child is about a week old, and I'm concerned about their eating and pooping habits. (*Starts crying.*) I just haven't been a parent very long and need to talk to someone, because I can't sleep.

ME. All right, let's get some information so I can verify this patient, and then I will page the parent concerns doctor on call.

Again, I don't have any kids. I'm sure there are some scary things involved with being a new parent, but many providers find it annoying and distracting to have to stop doing their hospital rounds to answer a call that could have waited until clinic hours. Unless the child is actively dying or doing something concerning, such as turning blue, vomiting, or having after-surgery complications, please wait until the daytime.

Sometime between 1:00 and 3:00 a.m. on a Saturday morning
ME. [Hospital]. This is Roxy.

PARENT OF PATIENT. Yes, my child is [between two and four months old], and I took their temperature using the forehead scanner, and it said 99.8, but I don't think that's accurate. So I used an underarm thermometer, and that said 100.2, but I don't think that's the most accurate either. So I woke my husband up, and we decided he should go to CVS to buy a rectal thermometer, and it said my child's temperature is 100.5. Can I please speak to a doctor on call about what to do?

I am fairly certain that *they* didn't decide to do that and that he wanted to stay home and sleep!

Approximately between ten o'clock and midnight on a Saturday night

ME. [Hospital]. This is Roxy.

THIRTY-YEAR-OLD FEMALE. I would like to speak with my dermatologist, please.

ME. Is this a medical emergency? Can you please give me a brief description of the issue?

THIRTY-YEAR-OLD FEMALE, *nonchalant.* Yes, I know I'm not supposed to, but I had a large zit on my cheek area near my mouth, and I popped it yesterday. It was fine until a couple of hours ago. Then it became red-streaked, swollen, and hurt to touch. The internet says it's infected. I know I shouldn't have done it, but normally, I don't have any problem when I pop the small ones. I just need some antibiotics called in to clear this up.

ME. Hold on while I page the doctor on call for you.

Don't pop your zits, y'all, no matter how tempting it is to get rid of them. Your mother was right: it will become infected. My own mother felt vindicated when I told her this story.

Between 2:00 and 6:00 a.m. on a Sunday morning

ME. [Hospital]. This is Roxy.

PATIENT'S FAMILY MEMBER. My [relative] has been passing out all night and having breathing problems. (*Goes into five-minute-long story that ends in crying.*) We went to [affiliated hospital thirty minutes away], but they keep saying nothing is wrong with her, and they are going to discharge her, but she passed out again in the ER while waiting to be discharged! Can I speak to a pulmonologist on call to see what to do?

ME, *perturbed.* I'm sorry—did you say that you are currently at a different hospital?

PATIENT'S FAMILY MEMBER. Yes! She's waiting to be discharged, and I wanted a second opinion.

ME. Unfortunately, since you are currently at a medical facility, I cannot page a doctor for you. You have the most available medical resources at your disposal currently. If the patient were to be discharged and this issue happened again in a home situation, I could page a doctor on call for you.

PATIENT'S FAMILY MEMBER. OK, I'll call back once she is discharged!

Forty-five minutes later

ME. [Hospital]. This is Roxy.

PATIENT'S FAMILY MEMBER. My [relative] has been passing out all night and having breathing problems. (*Goes into a five-minute-long story that ends in crying.*) She passed out again on the drive home after being discharged from the ER! Can I speak to a pulmonologist on call to see what to do?

ME, *starting to remember.* Did you call earlier?

PATIENT'S FAMILY MEMBER. Yes! I need to speak with a doctor now.

ME. OK, let me page the doctor on call for you.

Two minutes later

ME. [Direct doctor line]. This is Roxy.

PULMONOLOGIST. This is Dr. [Chief Resident]. You paged?

ME. Yes, I have an odd situation. A patient was seen at [affiliated hospital thirty minutes away] earlier tonight for issues with passing out and breathing difficulties, but the hospital discharged the patient. The patient passed out again in the car on the way home, and the relative has called in, asking what to do. I'll stay on the line to see if we need to connect to the transfer line.

PULMONOLOGIST. I'm not really sure how I can help besides telling them to come here, but go ahead and connect me.

ME, *to patient's family member and doctor.* You two should be connected.

PATIENT'S FAMILY MEMBER, *hysterically sobbing.* Hi, Doctor. This is [relative] of [patient]. I just don't know what to do. (*Gives fifteen-minute-long monologue of patient's entire history and relative's concerns and fears over not knowing what to do.*)

PULMONOLOGIST. At this point in the night, the only thing I can suggest to you is that you bring the patient here, and we can evaluate them in person in our ER.

PATIENT'S FAMILY MEMBER. We live in [an area thirty-five minutes away] and don't want to drive that far. Can you do a direct transfer and send an ambulance here?

PULMONOLOGIST. [Direct doctor line], can we do that?

ME. Unfortunately, if your relative is in that much medical distress, an ambulance would take them directly to the closest ER, which is the hospital you just left. If you want them transferred here, you can either drive the patient here yourself or discuss with the other ER doctor and have them do a direct admit to our hospital.

PATIENT'S FAMILY MEMBER. OK, we will go back to [other hospital]'s ER. (*Hangs up.*)

Thirty seconds later

ME. [Direct doctor line]. This is Roxy.

PULMONOLOGIST, *bewildered and slightly amused.* This is the doctor who was just on the line. Did that really just happen?

ME. Sunday mornings are weird.

PULMONOLOGIST. I don't do a lot of transfers in the middle of the night. Can we do that?

ME. Typically, no. (*Explains patient transfer admission process.*)

PULMONOLOGIST. That's what I thought. How far away do they live? I don't know the area too well.

ME. Google says they live about thirty to forty-five minutes away, but I've made that drive in thirty-eight minutes.

PULMONOLOGIST. Why don't they just drive here?

ME. I really don't know.

PULMONOLOGIST. OK, I'm going to ask my attending to see what we are supposed to do in this case if they call back.

ME. They probably will call back.

One hour later

ME. [Hospital]. This is Roxy.

PATIENT'S FAMILY MEMBER. This is [relative] of [patient], and we were just discharged again from the ER at [affiliated hospital thirty minutes away], and I don't know what to do. They won't let us transfer her, and I don't even know if they tried to transfer her.

ME. OK, I will page the doctor on call, and we will call the transfer line to see what's going on, and then I will call you back.

PATIENT'S FAMILY MEMBER. Thank you! I'll be waiting by the phone.

ME. [Direct doctor line]. This is Roxy.

PULMONOLOGIST. This is Dr. [Chief Resident]. Is it about the same patient?

ME. Yes.

PULMONOLOGIST. (*Lets out a heavy sigh.*) OK, let's go through the chart and see what's going on.

ME. I'm just going to put you on hold while I get the transfer line connected and see if the hospital actually did contact us.

TRANSFER LINE. This is Debra.

ME. Yes, this is the other [direct doctor line]. I have Dr. [Chief Resident] on the phone, and we have a weird situation. A patient's family member wants to have the patient directly admitted to our ER, but [affiliated hospital thirty minutes away] keeps discharging them. Can you see if the other hospital has tried to contact you to have the patient transferred here?

TRANSFER LINE. Let's see. It looks like they actually contacted us about two hours ago, but the [general medicine] doctor denied a direct admit.

PULMONOLOGIST. So what does that mean for us?

TRANSFER LINE. Unless they come through our ER or take a serious downturn, we can't directly admit them into our hospital tonight. They are more than welcome to come to our ER to see if our doctors have a different opinion about admitting them, but it most likely won't happen.

PULMONOLOGIST. I'm going to put that in my notes and pass that along to day shift.

ME. Me too. I have extensively documented this call, and my supervisor is aware, in case the relative calls back during the day. I'll go ahead and call the relative back to let them know what the decision was.

PULMONOLOGIST. Excellent. So we are all agreed on what to do. Thanks, everyone.

Two minutes later

ME. [Hospital]. I am calling for [patient's relative].

PATIENT'S FAMILY MEMBER. This is she.

ME. I just spoke with both the pulmonologist and the transfer line, and they informed me they won't be able to do a direct admit today for this patient unless you directly come through our ER and are evaluated here.

PATIENT'S FAMILY MEMBER, *upset and near tears again.* I just can't drive that far. If I call back later, do you think they could admit her?

ME. I don't normally work day shift, so I'm not sure what they would or would not be able to do on a Sunday afternoon, but you are more than welcome to call and ask later today.

PATIENT'S FAMILY MEMBER. OK, I'll do that.

I proceeded to send my supervisor and all the people working on day shift that Sunday an email to tell them that the attending pulmonologist, the transfer line, the pulmonologist on call, and I had agreed the patient could not be directly admitted to our hospital unless she walked into our ER to be evaluated. My overall time spent on the phone with this patient was seventy-eight minutes. The final resolution was "Just come to our ER." If this patient's relative had just driven to our ER at two o'clock in the morning, when they first called, the issue would have been resolved by four o'clock. Instead, we were all still discussing it at five o'clock. The family member ended up calling back at four o'clock in the afternoon and was again told to just come to our ER.

ME. [Hospital]. This is Roxy.

OLDER MALE, *voice filled with concern and a little bit of fear.* My wife has lady cancer. She just fainted, and I want to bring her there, but I want to talk to someone to see if she can be admitted and stay in the hospital, because she has appointments this week, and I don't think driving the hour there and back will be good for her. See, she's in her fifties and isn't supposed to be bleeding anymore, but y'all put one of them IEDs up in her to help stop the cancer, and I think that's messing with her blood pressure, because she keeps fainting. I don't know what to do. She's the only thing I have in this world, and I can't lose my wife.

ME. Sir, let me just look up her chart, and I can page the doctor on call for you.

OLDER MALE. Thank you, thank you, thank you.

ME. OK, I have the ob-gyn oncologist on the phone, and you two are connected.

DOCTOR. Sir, what's going on?

OLDER MALE. (*Explains the type of cancer his wife has and says we put an IED in her to stop the bleeding.*)

DOCTOR. OK, sir, if you bring her in, we can try to get her admitted and help her.

33

I loved this man; he was cute. He called back many times during the week to check on his wife, and he even called to have a nurse find the woman's glasses because she needed them for everything. Apparently, she was so out of it that she fell asleep with them in her breast pocket.

CHAPTER 5
I (Don't) Get Off on You

It took almost a year for my first sexual call to come in through my line. Apparently, to some, there is something appealing about calling a weekend night-shift hospital worker to say sexual things. I personally don't get it. I don't want to kink-shame, but this is a weird fetish, and I don't have time for it. Sorry for this chapter, Dad—feel free to skip ahead.

The following call came at 5:38 a.m. on a Sunday morning. I was ready to go home and go to sleep.

Me. [Hospital]. This is Roxy.

Female or high-pitched male patient. Yes, I have a question.

Me. Sure, how can I help?

Female or high-pitched male patient. I'm having some issues with my pussy.

Me, *not seeing any red flags yet because many people use expletives to describe scenarios and situations.* Have you been seen by a doctor about this before?

Female or high-pitched male patient. No.

Me. OK, let me transfer you to the emergency room.

Two minutes later

ME. [Hospital]. This is Roxy.

FEMALE OR HIGH-PITCHED MALE PATIENT. Yes, honey, I have a question that I need help with.

ME. (*Recognizes the number and realizes I'm going to have to be more customer-service-oriented.*) How can I help?

FEMALE OR HIGH-PITCHED MALE PATIENT. Yes, my pussy has been burning and tingling ever since my boyfriend fucked me last night. It's tingled before, but it hasn't burned like this.

ME, *with no mental alarm bells going off yet because people swear.* OK, well, we would suggest you either go to the emergency room right now if the pain is unbearable, or you can wait until seven o'clock, when the urgent care opens up.

FEMALE OR HIGH-PITCHED MALE PATIENT. Do you think it is weird that this happened? Has this happened to you? Does your pussy burn when your boyfriend fucks you?

ME. I'm not a licensed medical professional, so I can't advise on a problem like this.

FEMALE OR HIGH-PITCHED MALE PATIENT. Oh, honey, I understand. Let me just ask you one more question. How many fingers can you fit into your sweet pussy? (*Heavy breathing and masturbation sounds in the background.*)

ME, *stunned.* These calls are all recorded.

FEMALE OR HIGH-PITCHED MALE PATIENT. Oh, baby, you know you like it. You like when I ask questions. Just tell me how many fingers you can fit into your sweet pussy. (*Heavy breathing and masturbation sounds in the background.*)

ME. (*Immediately transfers call to security.*)

Between 2:00 and 4:00 a.m. on a Sunday

ME. [Hospital]. This is Roxy.

YOUNG ADULT FEMALE. Yes, so I have a question. My boyfriend and I just finished having sex, and I am twenty-four weeks pregnant, and I noticed that it hurt more than normal. Can I speak to a doctor? (*Sounds of male finishing and getting dressed in the background.*)

ME. I'm sorry, but what is it you are worried about?

YOUNG ADULT FEMALE. I am worried we might have hurt the baby or caused some issues.

ME. Hold on while I page a doctor.

ME. [Direct doctor line]. This is Roxy.

OB-GYN. Yes, I was paged.

ME. Yeah, I am really sorry about this phone call, but at least you will have a good story to tell your friends.

OB-GYN, *with a big sigh.* This can't be worse than the time I was paged at three in the morning on a Wednesday because the eighteen-year-old girl didn't know what an orgasm felt like, and I had to explain it to her.

ME, *shocked.* I'm sorry—what?

OB-GYN, *with sarcasm.* It was a great day.

ME. Well, this is a different situation. (*Explains situation.*) But aren't you glad you went to medical school to help people and babies?

OB-GYN, *probably wishing he picked a different specialty.* Oh yeah, this is exactly what I imagined.

On a Friday night around seven thirty

COWORKER. [Hospital]. How can I help you?

FEMALE SENIOR CITIZEN. Yes, I need to speak to an ob-gyn on call.

COWORKER. OK, can you give me a brief description of what's going on?

FEMALE SENIOR CITIZEN. I have excessive air in my hoo-ha, and that can't be good!

COWORKER. How do you know it's excessive?

FEMALE SENIOR CITIZEN. It just is, and I am having an emergency and need to talk to the doctor!

COWORKER, *holding back laughter.* I'm sorry, ma'am, but that's not a medical emergency, and I won't be able to page a doctor for you.

On a Friday night around eight o'clock

COWORKER. [Hospital]. How can I help you?

FREQUENT CALLER. Yes, I need to speak to my psychologist.

COWORKER. OK, can you give me a brief description of what's going on?

FREQUENT CALLER. Well, I am having married feelings, and I live alone, so I can't be having those feelings, and I need to be admitted to the hospital so they can figure out what's wrong with my head!

COWORKER. Are you in any pain or bleeding anywhere that you need to have a doctor look at you?

FREQUENT CALLER. No, but I am having thoughts about a man in a movie, and I live alone, and I can't be having these thoughts since I am alone. I need psychiatric help!

COWORKER. I'm sorry, ma'am, but that's not a medical emergency, and I won't be able to page a doctor for you.

CHAPTER 6
Scariest Moments of My Life

As I got more used to the routine of night shift, I became more relaxed and comfortable in my role. However, the karma gods seemingly took that as a challenge, as that was when I started receiving some of the scariest phone calls of my life. In the phone operator role, we weren't expected to do much besides connect patients to doctors, as extensive and specialized training in certain areas, such as psychology, was not provided. For a while, I thought I could somewhat predict what a call was going to be about, but I learned that the more experience I had, the less I knew. Fortunately, I was great at sounding official and making up quick answers to help defuse situations.

Approximately four o'clock on a Sunday morning
ME. [Hospital]. This is Roxy.
ADULT MALE. Yeah, I'm calling to let you know I'm going to blow up the hospital.
ME. Hold on while I transfer you to security.

Approximately five minutes later

ME. [Hospital]. This is Roxy.

ADULT MALE. Bitch, you transferred me to security. I'm going to blow you and this hospital up. What the fuck? You wish you could suck on the big, fat black cock before you die, you worthless bitch.

ME, *a little scared.* All these calls are recorded.

ADULT MALE. Good. Then you can get off on me saying—

ME. (*Transfers call back to security.*)

Between ten o'clock and midnight sometime

ME. [Hospital]. This is Roxy.

FEMALE PATIENT. The police told me to contact y'all to set up getting a rape kit done.

ME, *internally. What the hell?*

ME, *out loud.* OK, so you can just come into the ER and request a SANE [sexual assault nurse examiner] nurse. They should be able to help.

FEMALE PATIENT. OK, how does this procedure work?

I spent five minutes explaining the process as best as I understood it from TV shows and Google. I'll spare the details, but this woman was very open about what had happened. Hopefully she got the help she needed.

CHAPTER 7
Doctor's without Manners

Doctors are great—let's start with that. Doctors are helpful. Doctors will help save mankind, and they want to save people going through tough times. That being said, some doctors have God complexes and think they are better than everyone else. I get it: if I had the capabilities to save a life or fix a complex medical issue, I might start to get cocky too. But I think some people turn in their kindness and humanity to become doctors, and they have zero issues with trying to put others in what they think is their place.

This chapter is dedicated to all the doctors who thought they knew how to do my job, thought I was wrong, and proceeded to tell me so. To help with understanding the medical doctor hierarchy, here is a general ranking of how doctors are classified, how many years of schooling they have at each point, and my personal opinion of their abilities and experience.

- Intern: First year of residency program after graduating from medical school. They get shuffled around to the different specialties. They have approximately eight years of college and higher education so far. They usually are early to midtwenties, typically have zero experience with patients, and should not be trusted with much. Especially don't give them the on-call pager.

- Junior resident: Second year of residency program. They are still being shuffled around. These residents have had approximately eight to ten years of higher education and practice. They have seen some stuff, know a handful of things, and can sort of handle middle-of-the-night emergencies, but they usually have to ask someone higher up. They can occasionally be trusted with the on-call pager.
- Senior or chief resident: Third and fourth years of residency. They are starting to pick which general specialty they want to work with and are stable in their practice of medicine. They have approximately eight to twelve years of higher education and practice. They can be moderately trusted with the on-call pager and know most of the answers, but patients are great at coming up with difficult questions.
- Fellow: A person who has completed the four years of residency and has decided to go into a more advanced specialty and will require more specific training to become a better doctor. This doctor has been in school for a minimum of twelve to sixteen years, has seen many things, and has practiced specialized medicine. They should know what they're doing and are supposedly trustworthy with the on-call pager.
- Attending: The smartest of the smart. They know everything and have been crowned as the boss of everyone else to pass their wisdom down to. They have completed residency and, most likely, a fellowship, so they have a minimum of sixteen years of schooling and practice and are in their midthirties to forties or older. They are supposed to answer the on-call pager and know everything, but they are very busy and don't like to be bothered. In my experience, they do not always speak to me with kind words and sweet thoughts.

Approximately three thirty in the morning on a Friday

ME. [Direct doctor line]. This is Roxy.

CARDIAC DOCTOR. Yes, this is Dr. [Fellow].

ME. Fantastic. I have a doctor from another hospital who needs to speak with you.

CARDIAC DOCTOR, *very brusque.* I'm just a fellow; I don't think I should be answering these calls.

ME, *annoyed.* OK, well, you are the only person on call for cardiology. Is there someone else I can page instead of you?

CARDIAC DOCTOR. No, it's just me, but I really don't think I am qualified to work on these calls.

ME. OK, well, one of us went to medical school, and it wasn't me, so I think you're more qualified to help this person than I am.

CARDIAC DOCTOR. I will take the call, but I just don't think I should be answering these calls.

ME. (*Transfers call and immediately bangs head on desk.*)

I am still surprised to this day that this doctor didn't report me for talking back.

ME. [Direct doctor line]. This is Roxy.

GENERAL RESIDENT. Yeah, I'm just an intern, so I shouldn't be answering these calls. You'll have to call my attending to get help. (*Hangs up.*)

ME, *to myself. Then why are you number one on my call schedule? Why did they give you a pager?* (*Proceeds to page the chief resident on call, who I know is standing next to the intern.*) [Direct doctor line]. This is Roxy.

CHIEF RESIDENT. This is [doctor]. Is this about the patient you paged my intern for?

ME. Yes, why are they on my call schedule?

CHIEF RESIDENT. I don't know, but let's help this patient.

ME. [Direct doctor line]. This is Roxy.

NURSE ON CALL. Yes, you paged.

ME. Hi. I have a patient with [a neurology issue], and it says you're the first person to contact after hours, but I'm not sure if this is something you are allowed to handle.

NURSE ON CALL. It looks like a neurosurgery problem, and you would be better off speaking to the neurosurgeon on call; he will know more.

ME. OK, do you know who that is?

NURSE ON CALL. It's Dr. [Neurosurgeon], and he is actually sitting next to me.

ME. All right, I will send a page to him.

Ten minutes later, the neurosurgeon on call responded.

ME. [Direct doctor line]. This is Roxy.

NEUROSURGEON. Is this about the patient you just spoke with a nurse about?

ME. Yes.

NEUROSURGEON. OK, what was the problem again? She told me, but I wasn't listening.

ME. ...

I will never understand why doctors don't just pass the phone off to the right person if they are sitting right next to him or her.

ME. [Direct doctor line]. This is Roxy.

SURGERY ATTENDING. This is Dr. [Attending].

ME. Great. I have [another hospital] on the line. They need a surgery consult on a patient who was released today.

SURGERY ATTENDING. Why are you paging me? I'm not on call.

ME, *trying my hardest to remain respectful.* OK, well, according to the way I was trained, you are the person on call.

SURGERY ATTENDING. Walk me through what you did. I'm supposed to be backup and shouldn't be paged.

ME. (*Explains process.*)

SURGERY ATTENDING. No, you should have done it like this. (*Explains different process that is not in my training guideline or our 24-7 operating procedure and lectures me for eight minutes on how I'm doing my job wrong.*) You should really be asking your nursing supervisor how to do your job correctly. I shouldn't be explaining this.

ME, *frustrated because I am the only one in the department working these hours.* Great. I will do that when she is in the office on Monday. But thank you for informing me on what I did wrong, so I will know for the future. Should I page someone else to help me with this patient?

SURGERY ATTENDING. No, I'm here now. What is it?

ME. Well, this is a patient you were the attending for, you performed the surgery today, and the patient is currently in the ER at another hospital due to surgical complications.

SURGERY ATTENDING. Oh.

ME. [Direct doctor line]. This is Roxy.

SPECIALIST. This is [doctor].

ME. Yes, I have a doctor from [a different hospital], and they need a consult with you, please.

SPECIALIST, *assuming she is high and mighty.* No, it is not a consult; it is advice.

ME. OK, they need to speak with you about a patient. Hold on while I connect you.

It was about two o'clock in the morning, and I needed to page a doctor about a patient with a cardiology issue from another hospital.

ME. [Direct doctor line]. This is Roxy.

CARDIOLOGY FELLOW. Why did you page me?

ME. I have another hospital needing a consult about [a cardiology procedure].

CARDIOLOGY FELLOW. I am not on call for that. You need to page an attending. (*Hangs up.*)

At that point, I had to go through six different cardiology specialties to try to guess which attending I should contact. I didn't know the differences in the vague descriptions of the specialties, which were categorized by colors.

ME. [Direct doctor line]. This is Roxy.

CARDIOLOGY ATTENDING. This is [doctor].

ME. I have another hospital needing a consult about [a cardiology procedure].

CARDIOLOGY ATTENDING. OK, I'll take it.

Five minutes later

ME. [Direct doctor line]. This is Roxy.

CARDIOLOGY ATTENDING, *annoyed but holding it together.* Why did you page me? This should have gone to [different-colored cardiology specialty]. I have multiple procedures in the morning, and I need my sleep; it's not fair that the other doctors on call get to sleep, and I'm getting paged for things I'm not supposed to.

ME, *apologetic.* I'm sorry. My procedure tells me to page the attending, and I don't know the differences between the cardiology specialty colors. Is there someone else I should have contacted, so I can know for the future?

CARDIOLOGY ATTENDING. You did the right thing, but I'm confused why I was paged; there are other people who specialize in this. Do you have a supervisor I can talk to?

ME. (*Connects the doctor with the other direct doctor line and mutes my line.*)

CARDIOLOGY ATTENDING. (*Repeats the story to person who isn't actually my boss, doesn't control what I do, and has a different job title. Spends ten minutes complaining about being woken up and not being able to get enough sleep for his scheduled procedures in the morning and about my inability to know the difference between the different levels. I end up almost in tears while listening.*)

The overall outcome? I wasn't in trouble, and the man spent nearly twenty minutes of his life complaining about something that had taken him a total of two minutes to do on the phone. I don't think I was the one contributing to his lack of sleep at that point!

The following doctor surprised me and was amazing, and I want to marry into his family!

Approximately ten o'clock on a Friday night

ME. [Hospital]. This is Roxy.

HOME HEALTH NURSE, *nervous.* Yes, I have a ten-year-old with severe pulmonary problems, and I need to speak to the doctor on call.

He's going to be so annoyed, because I called about an hour ago, and I'm already bothering him again.

ME. OK, can you briefly describe what is going on?

HOME HEALTH NURSE. [The medical equipment operator] wants a faxed copy of the doctor's orders and won't let me change the settings using the electronic orders that this doctor sent.

ME. What?

HOME HEALTH NURSE. They want a physical copy of the orders.

ME. Is there anyone in that office to accept a copy right now?

HOME HEALTH NURSE. No, and I can't get a hold of the on-call person. This kid really needs the settings changed.

ME. Let me page the doctor on call.

ME. [Direct doctor line]. This is Roxy.

DOCTOR. Yes, this is [pediatric pulmonologist].

ME. Yes, I have a home health nurse who needs a physical copy of the patient's equipment orders faxed to the office right now.

DOCTOR, *shocked*. What!

ME. Hold on while I connect you.

At that point, I put them on mute and proceeded to listen to the conversation because I wanted to hear the resolution.

DOCTOR. This is [pediatric pulmonologist].

HOME HEALTH NURSE, *apologetic*. Yes, the [equipment office] won't accept electronic orders, and they aren't allowing me to change the settings without the on-call person there. This kid is having issues breathing, and I need to fix the settings on the [machine].

DOCTOR. Didn't I already send over the orders?

HOME HEALTH NURSE. Yes, but they don't accept electronic orders. They want a physical copy written on a prescription pad.

DOCTOR, *sounding fed up with the situation*. It is 2020. I don't even have physical prescription pads anymore. Everything is electronic. We don't even have access to a fax machine after-hours. We have one machine, and it is locked up in a room that I don't even have access to. What is this company's name?

HOME HEALTH NURSE. It is [company]. They have been difficult to work with. Their on-call person won't allow me to change the settings. I need to always have one of their representatives physically with me to change the settings. I asked if the parents could take a class and learn how to adjust the settings themselves, but they yelled at me and said no one except a licensed physician is allowed to mess with the settings. The parents are really stressed that they can't fix the settings themselves and have to wait for someone to come help their child.

DOCTOR, *concerned.* What company did you say this was again?

HOME HEALTH NURSE. [Company].

DOCTOR, *calm but definitely seething internally.* OK, I will personally call their management team on Monday to cancel our contract with them. There are classes that we encourage parents to take to help prevent these situations, and it is absolutely not true that you need to be supervised to change the settings. How far away does the patient live?

HOME HEALTH NURSE. About forty-five minutes away.

DOCTOR. OK, tomorrow is Saturday. I want you to have the parents come in, and I will personally show them how to change the settings. If the machine isn't working properly or doing what it should, I will swap that machine out with a different one until the clinics open up again on Monday, and we can find a new company. This absolutely should not be happening, and this isn't the first problem we've had with them. You call back with any problems before tomorrow. I will be dealing with [company] on Monday. Have a good night.

I love when doctors actually want to find solutions and aren't bothered by somewhat minor issues.

CHAPTER 8
Don't You Know There's a Pandemic, Charlie Brown?

During March 2020, the coronavirus pandemic swept America. Fortunately, I was lucky enough to be considered an essential worker, which meant extra shifts but a reliable paycheck. During the first weekend of the dreaded COVID-19 crisis, I worked thirty-one hours between Friday at 9:00 p.m. and Sunday at 10:00 p.m., taking a total of four hundred calls. In the height of the pandemic, in July and August, each person at the call center could expect up to four hundred phone calls in a six-hour shift. About 75 percent of the calls were related to COVID-19. For reference, I normally took a total of 120 calls in a twenty-hour work weekend or 80 calls in a six-hour shift during the daytime. And let me reiterate: I am not a licensed medical professional, but everyone was calling my workplace for answers. I did not have them. I understand that the new medical mystery sweeping the world was confusing, upsetting, and out of control, but as someone who was unexpectedly one of the main people fielding phone calls, I just wanted everyone to go home and be quiet. In the words of Taylor Swift, "You need to calm down."

In case you weren't lucky enough to be an essential worker, allow me to sum up how people saw us: essential workers now knew all the answers. In reality, essential workers were making it up on the fly. I made up a lot. The first week of the main scare, people would call to cancel appointments or ask to see loved ones, or they assumed the coronavirus would immediately kill them as soon as they touched hospital property. Later, people drifted toward being mad and angry that security and hospital administrators wouldn't allow visitors during the crisis.

After a couple of weeks, the hospital created many new rules, which apparently were difficult for some to follow. One of the biggest rules was that there could only be one visitor per patient per day from noon to 7:00 p.m. The hospital also closed the waiting rooms and restricted entrance into the hospitals, which, in my opinion, was smart. Hospitals are notoriously germy and the site of many infections. In my medical microbiology class, we spent three weeks learning about hospital-specific illnesses and diseases that travel among patients and hospitals. Frankly, you should avoid any extended time in a hospital.

Another new rule was that anyone who could work from home worked from home. Fortunately and unfortunately, I got to work from home, which meant setting up a desk (just a folding card table) in my bedroom closet, about ten feet from my bed. Let me tell you, working the night shift is hard when you just want to curl up in bed and ignore a pandemic. Fortunately, my cat is chatty and liked to help answer the phone. She is now a licensed medical professional and will be referred to as Dr. Tatiana. If anyone heard her medical advice, I am sorry that she wanted to help. She probably has better medical answers than I do.

After answering so many phone calls, I stopped giving people my name, because some people wrote it down and added it to their list of people to sue about their family members' care. My job was not that important, and they didn't need to know who I was.

The following phone calls were the types of pandemic-specific calls my coworkers and I received.

The first weekend of the crisis brought calls like the following:

ME. [Hospital]. This is Roxy.

PATIENT. Yes, I'd like to cancel my upcoming appointment.

ME. (*Gets patient info.*) OK, can I get a reason why you are canceling?

PATIENT REASON ONE. Well, I'm just trying to cancel all nonurgent appointments for the immediate future.

PATIENT REASON TWO. I'm scared of that virus that's out there.

PATIENT REASON THREE. I'm elderly and very at risk, so I'd rather not leave my house unless it is for a dire emergency.

PATIENT REASON FOUR. My kids aren't going back to school, and I have to stay at home to watch them for a while and can't leave them alone while I go to an appointment.

This specific interaction happened at least ten times in one day:

ME. [Hospital]. This is Roxy.

PATIENT. Yes, I'd like to cancel my upcoming appointment.

ME. (*Gets patient info.*) Can I get a reason why you are canceling?

PATIENT. Well, I don't want to risk getting that corona.

ME. I see this is a chemotherapy appointment.

PATIENT. Yes, I have stage-three cancer.

ME. OK, you will have to call back during the week to reschedule that appointment, because oncology doctors are very strict with appointments.

PATIENT. OK, dear. Thanks. (*Hangs up.*)

ME, *thinking to myself. Sir, you have cancer. Your body is dying. You absolutely have to come get treatment.*

ME. [Hospital]. This is Roxy.

PATIENT. Yes, I have a question about my husband's upcoming appointment.

ME. (*Gets patient info*.) I see this is a chemotherapy appointment.

PATIENT. Yes, I am worried he will get corona while he is in the hospital for his chemo treatment

ME, *breathing heavily to keep calm*. If he becomes ill, our doctors will be there to help him, and there are a lot of cleaning protocols in place.

ME, *thinking to myself. No, we're just going to let your sick husband die in our care. That's what doctors do.*

This one is on me, but let me explain. I ran out of patience and was tired of stupid questions. I had also answered four hundred back-to-back calls in less than six hours. I'm surprised it took me that long before I snapped.

The following happened at approximately four thirty on a Monday afternoon, three days into the official pandemic.

ME, *out of patience*. [Hospital]. How can I help you?

PATIENT. Hello. Who am I speaking with?

ME. [Hospital]. How can I help you?

PATIENT. I don't even get to know the person I am speaking with? I would like to know your name before we continue.

ME, *heavy with attitude and annoyance*. This is Roxy. What do you want?

PATIENT. Well, hello, Roxy. How are you doing on this blessed day?

ME. Fine. How can I help you?

PATIENT. Well, aren't you in a rush? What's the hurry? We have all the time we need.

ME. Is there a medical issue I can help you with?

PATIENT. Yes, I have a mammogram appointment in two weeks, and I was wondering if I could bring two people with me to that appointment. (*Starts to explain why and give more details than I need.*)

ME. Hold on while I transfer you to that department. (*Transfers call.*)

COWORKER. [Hospital].

ADULT MOTHER. My son has swallowed razorblades.

COWORKER. You need to take him to the ER right now.

ADULT MOTHER. But what if he gets coronavirus in the ER?

COWORKER. He will die of internal bleeding before he gets coronavirus. Hang up, and call 911 now.

Sadly, I don't believe this woman took her son to the ER, but I hope he is OK.

At about 11:20 on a Saturday night in June

ME. [Hospital]. This is Roxy.

ADULT MALE. I need to talk to a social worker or a care advocate, please.

ME. Is this an emergency? The office is closed until Monday.

ADULT MALE. Well, I am concerned that my doctors are racist and don't like me. (*Goes on a five-minute-long rant about his experience at certain doctors' offices and how he thinks he has been discriminated against.*)

ME. Sir, I don't think this is an emergency. You will have to call back.

ADULT MALE, *getting mad.* Then why did you make me explain all that?

ME, *trying to defuse the situation.* I just needed a brief explanation.

ADULT MALE. Well, I would consider this an emergency. You know, with all the Black Lives Matter stuff, now is not a good time to be pissing off a black man.

ME. Was that a threat?

ADULT MALE. It wasn't a threat, but I want y'all to know I am serious that I think the doctors aren't giving me adequate care.

ME. OK, well, the office that can take care of that will open up on Monday.

ADULT MALE. I know. I already have a caseworker and a case number, but I want this dealt with now.

ME. ...

The following call occurred in November 2020, during the second wave of the pandemic.

ME. [Hospital]. This is Roxy.

ADULT FEMALE, *nicely.* Yes, I know there are visitor regulations, but I was wondering if my husband could come with me to my three cancer appointments on Monday. We are going to go over next steps and care of life, and he needs to be there for that.

ME, *genuinely wanting to help.* That's a good question, and I'm not really sure. I know we make exceptions for end-of-life, physically disabled, and mentally disabled persons, who are allowed to have one caretaker come in with them.

ADULT FEMALE. No, I'm still physically able to support myself, and I am sound of mind, but he really does need to be there.

ME. Unfortunately, that office is closed for the day, but if you can call back during business hours, they'd be able to give you a better answer. I'm sorry I couldn't give you a more specific answer.

ADULT FEMALE. That's all right! That's better than what I thought you would say.

ME. If I was in your position, I would bring him in anyway, and if anyone says anything, then I would just fight a security guard. But I'm not in charge.

ADULT FEMALE. There's probably a reason for that.

The following types of calls happened far too frequently.

Between 10:00 p.m. and 4:00 a.m. on a weekend night

ME. [Hospital]. This is Roxy.

PATIENTS OF VARYING AGES. I found out three hours ago that my [roommate, relative, or best friend's cousin] is positive for the corona, and I want to be tested.

ME. Are you showing any active symptoms?

PATIENT. No, but I'm concerned because we were at a barbecue together.

ME. Unfortunately, we can't test you unless you come to the ER with active symptoms. You will have to wait until the Monday to call your primary care physician to schedule a test.

PATIENT, *gaining volume*. But I'm really concerned!

ME. I'm very sorry, but unless you are showing active symptoms, we cannot test you in the middle of the night. Is there anything else I can help you with?

PATIENT. No!

In case it comes up, there are a few tests that health care providers are willing to do in the middle of the night if you are not showing current symptoms or actively dying.

Around two o'clock in the morning on a Saturday night in August 2020

ME. [Hospital]. This is Roxy.

FEMALE VISITOR. Yes, I would like to make a complaint about your security in the ER.

ME. Can I get a brief description of the incident?

FEMALE VISITOR, *agitated*. They do not know the correct procedures in the ER, and the procedures keep changing. It's very unprofessional, and I can't call ahead to see what has changed, because they don't even know! My husband is in the ER, and I tried to bring him [something not very important or life-changing], and they wouldn't let me in with my six-month-old baby, but earlier today, I came in with my baby. I can't leave a six-month-old alone, and there's no one else who can watch her. Why doesn't security know the policies better? Why can't I just bring him [item] or have security pass it along to him?

ME. Ma'am, I am not sure, but I will page the house supervisor so they can open a line of investigation.

Why does anyone feel entitled to bring a six-month-old baby to an ER? I thought, *Why can't your husband wait until he is discharged to get the item? Why do you feel the need to make a complaint about our policies that change daily? It's the middle of the night in the middle of a pandemic. Stay home!*

In the beginning of January 2021, the COVID-19 vaccines started to become more widely available. In fact, this news was made public before the vaccine hotline was even set up or planned out thoroughly. That led to many calls like the following.

COWORKER. [Hospital]. How can I help you?

POTENTIAL PATIENT. I need the vaccine.

COWORKER. Unfortunately, at this point in time, we are not open to scheduling vaccines to the public. We suggest you follow local news or the CDC website to find out when the vaccine will be available.

POTENTIAL PATIENT, *trying to get their way immediately.* I saw on Facebook that it's available, so I want to get it now!

COWORKER. Unfortunately, we have not been given any information on when it will be available to the public, but if you follow the newspapers, you will be able to find out when it is available.

POTENTIAL PATIENT. (*Incoherent, angry grumbling.*)

Once the vaccine was made available, the vaccine hotline booked all the available appointments in one hour and forty-three minutes. Between one thousand and five thousand appointments were made with no idea of when the next shipments or appointments would start. The initial requirement for the general public to receive the vaccine was for an individual to be over sixty-five years of age. A day after all the appointments were booked, the requirement was changed to individuals over eighty years of age. The overwhelming desire for people to be vaccinated and the completely filled available appointment slots led to far too many calls like the following.

COWORKER. [Hospital]. How can I help you?

POTENTIAL PATIENT. I need the vaccine.

COWORKER. Unfortunately, at this point in time, we do not have any more available appointments, and we are unsure when we will get more appointments. You are welcome to call back next week or contact your local primary care provider to see if they can help coordinate getting you the vaccine.

POTENTIAL PATIENT. (*Incoherent, angry grumbling and usually a cycle that requires repeating the above statement at least three or four times before the potential patient hangs up.*)

EPILOGUE

Like all good things, this book must somehow come to an end. I'm sure I could keep working on this book forever and gather many more stories as I continue to work with the general public in a medical setting. However, I am choosing to immortalize the most memorable stories and keep the mediocre tales out of the spotlight.

This job was hard, and not every day was worth it. Some days, I was convinced our patients didn't have three brain cells among all of them combined. Many of my friends who heard these stories didn't even believe these conversations had actually happened. Believe me, though, these situations happened, and they all happened on a recorded line.

One of the few things that kept me going, as corny as it sounds, was the positive interaction I had with patients, such as the man whose wife had "lady cancer," as he called it. He brought a smile to my face and made me realize my job and my efforts made a difference in his life. The pediatric pulmonologist who went out of his way to help a small kid and his nurse made me happy that I got to work with doctors who truly wanted to help those in medical need. Whenever patients showed genuine gratitude and appreciation, I was thrilled to be at my job and helping people.

Even though this job is marketed as an easy job for students and those without an extensive medical background, I am convinced that anyone who works as any type of hospital call girl is a genius. The ability to decipher a patient's medical descriptions and translate that information to a doctor is not a simple task. I am also a firm believer that anyone who wants to work as a licensed medical professional should be required to work as a hospital call girl. This would allow future medical professionals to accurately understand what it is like to work with patients. Yes, doctors save lives and perform miracles, but I don't think medical newbies truly understand what it's like in the trenches.

In the end, I think my experience working as a hospital call girl taught me patience in a new way. It taught me how to keep all my panic inside and how to direct hysterical people in somewhat dire situations. I wouldn't say I'm a crisis expert now by any means, but I'm definitely better at handling other people's crises, or at the very least, I'm better at determining what an actual crisis is. This job tried my patience and my coping skills, but overall, it taught me skills I will use for the rest of my life. At the very least, the job gave me this book, and for that, it was all worth it.

Printed in the United States
by Baker & Taylor Publisher Services